SUBWAY LINE, No. 14

Philosophical Thinking is Yoga for the Mind®

PHILOSOPHICAL TRUFFLES

Michael Eskin

Upper West Side Philosophers, Inc.

New York

Published by Upper West Side Philosophers, Inc.,
P. O. Box 250645, New York, NY 10025.

The colophon is a registered trademark of Upper West Side
Philosophers, Inc.

Yoga for the Mind®

Library of Congress Cataloging-in-Publication Data

Names: Eskin, Michael, author.
Title: Philosophical truffles / Michael Eskin.
Description: New York : Upper West Side Philosophers, Inc.,
  2018. | Series: Subway line ; No. 14
Identifiers: LCCN 2017015858 | ISBN 9781935830528
  (pbk. : alk. paper)
Subjects: LCSH: Life--Quotations, maxims, etc. | Conduct
  of life--Quotations, maxims, etc. | Philosophy--Quotations,
  maxims, etc.
Classification: LCC BD431 .E89 2018 | DDC 191--dc23
LC record available at https://lccn.loc.gov/2017015858

CONTENTS

How to read this book / 13

~

1. On thinking and sadness / 15
2. On lying and truth / 16
3. On reinventing the wheel / 19
4. Why the adage 'history teaches
nothing' is and is not true / 20
5. On academics and why they are
dangerous / 23
6. On cowards / 25
7. On parents and children / 26
8. On power / 28
9. On fear / 29
10. On logic and life / 30
11. On enemies / 33
12. On nostalgia and regret / 34
13. On loving unconditionally / 35
14. On one's own voice,
contra academicos / 36
15. On freedom and pressure / 38
16. Gift and poison / 39

17. On getting old / 40
18. On the structure of prejudice / 41
19. On demanding love / 43
20. On fate in the digital age / 44
21. On divorce / 46
22. On marriage / 47
23. On tidal waves / 48
24. On being Jewish / 49
25. On a low point in philosophy / 50
26. On turning a blind eye / 51
27. On those who are out to get you / 52
28. On spousal loyalty / 53
29. On responsibility / 54
30. On Kant's definition of
    enlightenment / 55
31. On dialogue / 56
32. On love / 57
33. On the extra moron / 58
34. On fairness / 60
35. On lawyers / 61
36. On great philosophers / 62
37. On the iPhone / 63
38. Nomen est omen / 64

39. Geneva on the lake / 65
40. Julia Livilla upstate / 66
41. On the longevity of art / 67
42. On being right and being wrong / 68
43. On "I didn't mean it" / 69
44. On friends / 70
45. On novelty / 71
46. On firsts in philosophy / 72
47. On nonviolent communication / 73
48. America / 74
49. On revenge, *more cynico* / 75
50. On genius / 76
51. On aphorisms / 77
52. On simplicity without
simplification / 78
53. On a lamprey / 79
54. On the pursuit of ethics / 81
55. On being a philosopher / 82
56. On love II / 83
57. On marrying for money / 84
58. On intelligence and genius / 85
59. On winning and losing / 86
60. On wanting children / 87

61. On Republicans and Democrats / 88
62. On the wrong side of the bed / 89
63. On love and responsibility / 90
64. On aging / 91
65. On what the 'wise man' would do / 92
66. Why politicians lie ... / 93
67. On observing without judging / 95

~

About the Author / 99

THE TRUFFLES

Would it were possible to capture the world—
life, fate, human folly and human achieve-
ment—the small and the big things, sadness,
happiness, childhood and old age, music, poetry, love, friendship and hatred, and pain—in
one long aphorism!

(Marquis de Rossignol)

All men of whatever quality they be, who
have done anything of excellence, or which
may properly resemble excellence, ought, if
they are persons of truth and honesty, to de-
scribe their life with their own hand; but they
ought not to attempt so fine an enterprise till
they have passed the age of forty.

(Benvenuto Cellini)

How to read this book

The following aphorisms and essays on the most diverse subjects are not presented as truths but, rather, as snapshots of thinking intended to entertain and provoke thinking in turn. They should be examined, tested, falsified, enjoyed and, above all, savored: like truffles that gradually dissolve on our tongue, suffusing us with the gustatory memory of their transient shape and texture, and leaving us desiring more …

ON THINKING AND SADNESS

Some say that thinking makes you sad. What nonsense! If anything, thinking makes you realize that what *makes* you sad is *you*. Thinking is a most effective and lasting remedy for sadness.

On Lying and Truth

It is commonly held that lying is the opposite of telling the truth. Clearly, however, this cannot be the case, as it is possible not to tell the truth without lying at the same time. This misconception is based on the assumption that both lying and telling the truth belong to the same —declarative—category of speech. Lying and telling the truth are held to be two, diametrically opposed, modes of saying that something is or is not such and such, or that something is or is not the case.

While this assumption is certainly correct, it makes us all too easily forget that what makes a statement a lie is not a function of its grammatical structure but of its intentional, volitional, or dispositional thrust. In other words, an untrue statement becomes a lie not because it is not true, but because it was said with the intention or will to deceive. Not telling or speaking the truth is not equal to lying.

What is important about this realization is that it allows us to make a categorical distinction between lying and truth, which may in turn have important consequences for the way we deal with the question of truth and lying in the various domains of our lives: Lying falls within the purview of ethics, the question of truth falls within the purview of metaphysics or ontology. Lying bespeaks a certain disposition, volition, or stance toward the world and oneself; truth pertains to the way the world and everything in it is or is not.

Thus, we can reasonably teach or expect a person not to lie, but we cannot, at bottom, expect a person to tell or speak the truth, as 'truth', being a metaphysical

problem, will essentially remain unde-
cided.

ON REINVENTING THE WHEEL

In philosophy the wheel must constantly be reinvented. Knowing what others have thought is not (yet) thinking.

WHY THE ADAGE 'HISTORY TEACHES NOTHING' IS AND IS NOT TRUE

If we want to understand the significance of this much-invoked bit of proverbial wisdom we have to ask what 'teaches nothing' exactly means in this context. For, surely, it cannot simply mean what it says given that we can obviously learn, for instance, from past mistakes and hence from history, which is consequently capable of teaching us something.

In order to make sense of this adage, then, we have to examine its underlying assumptions.

The first assumption is that history is, at bottom, a negative process marked by suffering and violence—hence, the implied injunction to learn from history so as to do it better in the future. The second assumption is that the same bad things continue happening without any real sign of improvement. In light of these assumptions 'teaches nothing' would seem to suggest that we are incapable, on the whole, of making the world better.

This holds true only if we think of history as a zero-sum game played out between victims and perpetrators, whereby both sides learn how 'better' to do what they do, with the perpetrators always being one step ahead of the victims, as it were. The perpetrators get better at inflicting harm, the victims get better at withstanding the perpetrators' onslaughts —but never quite good enough to be able to fend them off completely. The net result remains the same. Thus, only from the impersonal viewpoint of divine objectivity would it be true to say that 'history teaches nothing'. From the perspective of individual life, this statement

can hardly be true, as we all can, and
sometimes do learn from the past, which
doesn't mean that we always know how
to put what we have learned to good use.

On academics and why they are dangerous

Academics can be divided into four kinds: those in whom extreme intelligence is coupled with a sense of (extreme) superiority; those in whom intelligence is coupled with a sense of inferiority; those in whom stupidity is coupled with a sense of (extreme) superiority; and, finally, all those in between. (Those in whom stupidity is coupled with inferiority could never make it in the academy.)

Those of the first kind are dangerous because they typically know what they want and how to get it; those of the second kind are dangerous because they tend to act on emotion rather than reason; those of the third kind are dangerous because they will act at any scheming flatterer's bidding and because they don't tolerate competition and criticism; those of the fourth kind are dangerous because they would do anything to be counted among the first.

On Cowards

Most people are cowards. They will watch you put yourself on the line and wait to see what happens. If you win, they will rally behind you. If you lose, they will keep a distance.

On parents and children

If we are lucky, our parents are, up to a certain point in our lives, our biggest supporters—the point at which we begin outgrowing them, thereby threatening the precarious equilibrium of their lives. If we are then lucky, they will not become our enemies.

~

Is friendship between parents and children possible? Friendship presupposes equality, and children and parents are never equals.

~

We owe our children everything and our parents nothing. To give ourselves to our children is an obligation, to give ourselves to our parents a gift.

~

It is particularly paralyzing to realize that
we may not be able to save our children
from themselves. We are at once both
Protagoras and Socrates—hoping that
virtue can be taught and suspecting that it
can't.

Power only works in the face of fear. It loses its force as soon as it is met with in-difference and courage.

~

Most of us are afraid of something most of the time.

ON FEAR

Those who instill fear end up fearing those who fear them.

—with W. H. Auden in mind

A well-known philosopher has recently suggested that "bullshit is a greater enemy of the truth than lies are" because unlike lying, which recognizes the "authority of the truth" in the very act of rejecting it, bullshit does not reject the authority of truth but simply "pays no attention to it at all." Bullshit is "neither on the side of the true nor on the side of the false." Unlike the "honest man and the liar," the bullshitter is not concerned at all with facts or truth. To the extent that the "authority of the truth" is the very core and foundation of our society, consequently, the bullshitter can be said to pose a greater threat to it than the liar: Bullshitting "constitutes a more insidious threat than lying does to the conduct of civilized life," insofar as it is rooted in truth.

The logic underlying this argument can be formalized roughly as follows: Not paying any attention to x at all, or not being concerned with x at all—whereby x is to be understood as the core and foundation of y—is a greater threat to (the viability of) y than outrightly rejecting x. Or, to put it differently: Outrightly denying the validity of x is a lesser threat to y than paying no attention to x at all.

On paper this may look like a sexy formula. In truth, however, this crude exercise in binary logic can easily be revealed as being itself a piece of 'bullshit' posing as a viable ethics. For, applied to real life, this argument would mean that those who pay no attention to us at all pose a greater threat to our life-world than those who explicitly reject us. On this logic, it would have been even worse for the Jews if the Nazis had paid no attention to them at all! What nonsense!

In the interest of survival, I suggest that we pay attention to those in particular who explicitly reject us and not worry about those who ignore us.

On a final note: Insofar as the bullshitter is as likely to say something that is true as something that is not true—having no grounds for choosing one or the other—shouldn't he be preferred to the (habitual) liar, who will, by definition, not tell the truth?

—in response to H. G. Frankfurt's
On Bullshit and *Truth*

Your greatest enemies are those whom you have seen in a moment of shame and who know that you saw them. They will never forgive you for it.

On Nostalgia and Regret

We pay a high price for both not following love and following what we mistake for love. The price of the latter is nostalgia, the price of the former regret.

ON LOVING UNCONDITIONALLY

Even those who love you unconditionally
have conditions—and they know it.

On one's own voice,
CONTRA ACADEMICOS

One of my favorite passages in philosophy is the following:

> And so a gathering like this of ours, when it includes such men as most of us claim to be, requires no extraneous voices, not even of the poets, whom one cannot question on the sense of what they say; when they are adduced in discussion we are generally told by some that the poet thought so and so, and by others, something different, and they go on arguing about a matter which they are powerless to determine. No, this sort of meeting is avoided by men of culture, who prefer to converse directly with each other, and to use their own way of speech in putting one another by turns to the test. It is this sort of person

that I think you and I ought rather to im-
itate.

~

We, academics, all too often hide behind
the words of others—preferably, dead
others—presuming to understand them
"better than they understood themselves," as a critic once put it. If Socrates'
final piece of advice to Alcibiades were to
become the equivalent of the Hippocratic
Oath for scholars in the humanities, our
colleges and universities would (can it be
hoped?) be staffed with fewer hypocrites
…

—in response to Plato, *Protagoras* 347e-348a
(Loeb classical edn., trans. W. R. M. Lamb)

On Freedom and Pressure

If you are free nobody can pressure you—even under pressure the decision is yours.

GIFT AND POISON

Metaphor and metonymy are a blessing and a curse: a gift—perhaps the greatest—as without them we would not be able to communicate; and poison—perhaps the deadliest—because they empower us to draw a line between those who shall live and those who shall die.

On getting old

You first realize that you are getting old
when you begin feeling that you would
like to be young again.

On the Structure of Prejudice

In logic, a distinction is commonly made between analytic and synthetic judgments. Both kinds of judgment are concerned with the relation between subject and predicate. In the case of analytic judgments, the predicate is considered part of the very concept of the subject; in the case of synthetic judgments, the predicate is considered external to the concept of the subject. From this it follows that analytic judgments are by definition not based on experience, while all judgments of experience are by definition synthetic. Thus, as Immanuel Kant explains, "all bodies are extended" is an analytic judgment because the very concept of 'body' implies extension, whereas "all bodies are heavy" is a synthetic judgment because the concept of 'body' does not imply 'being heavy'—this, according to Kant, can only be known from experience.

In light of the distinction between synthetic and analytic judgments, the structure of prejudice can be described as follows: A prejudice is an unverified synthetic judgment posing as an analytic judgment.

All too often, we allow ourselves to be duped by this logical masquerade—herein lies its perniciousness.

ON DEMANDING LOVE

When it comes to love, one of the most destructive things you can do is to demand the love that you are already receiving.

"Not even God himself can escape fate," the Delphic oracle is reported as saying to Croesus after his defeat by Cyrus.

Herodotus presents the story of the rise and fall of the Lydian empire under the Mermnadae, beginning with Gyges' usurpation of the throne and ending with the demise of his great-great-grandson, Croesus, at the hands of the Persians, as a cautionary tale about transgression and retribution: Gyges' crime—murdering king Candaules, stealing "his office, to which he had no claim," and marrying the queen—is decreed to be expiated in the fifth generation. The mode of expiation, as the Delphic oracle foretells Croesus, who misinterprets the prophecy, taking it to refer to the Persians, whom he is poised to attack: the destruction of a great empire—his own, as he is soon to find out.

Clicking the 'send' button and knowing, as you click it, that you shouldn't have sent the e-mail is as close as we come to experiencing fate in the digital age …

—in response to Herodotus, *Histories,* book 1

On divorce

The courage to want the other's pain without wanting it is as important as the courage to be true to oneself.

A good marriage isn't work: it works.

—with a widespread belief in mind

Only rarely, if at all, are we given the chance to change the course of our life: in the aftermath of a cataclysmic event, perhaps—or in those rare moments when life itself hits us like a tidal wave, flooding the shores of our being and hurling us into the truth of our future. Whether we choose to live by our truth, or whether we choose to betray it—there is no way back.

On being Jewish

What does it mean to be Jewish?—Depending on whom you talk to, being Jewish will be understood in racial, ethnic, national, cultural, or religious terms. Above all, however, being Jewish is a state of heart and mind.

On a low point in philosophy

The day when Martin Heidegger, president of the University of Freiburg, denied his teacher, Edmund Husserl, access to the university library because he was Jewish.

ON TURNING A BLIND EYE

To the extent that we turn a blind eye to the misdeeds of others if we stand to benefit from them, we are all opportunists.

On those who are out to get you

Those who are out to get you will always find a reason to find fault with what you do, no matter what you do. Trying to meet their expectations is utterly futile, as they expect you to fail one way or another.

On spousal loyalty

Never complain to one spouse about the other, unless you want to lose the friend-ship of both.

ON RESPONSIBILITY

Knowing where your responsibilities end
is as important as knowing what you are
responsible for.

—with Emmanuel Levinas in mind

On Kant's definition of enlightenment

Immanuel Kant defines enlightenment as our emergence from our self-imposed nonage. This implies that we must have already been enlightened before we imposed nonage on ourselves and, consequently, that the imposition of nonage on ourselves must have been an enlightened act. Why would we have given up being enlightened in the first place?

True dialogue is rare. More often than not, we talk *at* rather than *with* our interlocutors—what looks like dialogue is, in fact, bilateral monologue.

Love—whatever else it may be—is the realization that the other comes first.

On the Extra Moron

I was driving our friend, Moishe Mandelbaum, to Grand Central Station that morning. "There's always an extra moron in the street for you," he said, as I was pulling up to the curb at Vanderbilt Avenue and David Ben-Gurion Place and almost bumped into the cab in front of us—"including yourself!" he added. "That's good!" I said—"that's really good—did you come up with it?" "Yes," he said, "a long time ago."

I retrieved his backpack from the trunk, we said our good-byes, and he walked off. How much life, I thought to myself, as I was watching this seventy-six-year old immigrant from Lithuania cross

the street toward the Main Concourse,
goes into a good aphorism!

On fairness

Fairness is a tactical notion. What is and what is not considered fair depends on four factors: the situation, the parties involved, the framework of distributive justice in place, and those who have the power of decision. Because one can never be certain that the parties involved, or those who have the power of decision will be inclined toward fairness, it is fair to say that life is not fair.

On Lawyers

The real reason why lawyers have a bad reputation is neither because they are greedy and cannot be trusted nor because the world would, presumably, be a less litigious and, hence, better place without them, but because we are too disingenuous not to impute our own greediness, litigiousness and mendacity to them. Our lawyers are as greedy, litigious and mendacious as we ask them to be on our behalf.

What makes a philosopher great is his capacity philosophically to conjure an entire new world, which we in turn must imagine ourselves inhabiting in order to determine whether we like or dislike his philosophy.

ON THE iPhone

so much depends
upon

a small dotted
- i -

beside the Book
the Mac

the Pod and
the Phone …

… for it was made for you!

For J.-P. S.

Nomen est Omen

It may take a lifetime to free oneself of the superstitious belief that one's name is one's destiny. Why should it be? How could it be? After all, destiny has to do with fate, and fate has to do with the gods, and chances are that the gods had nothing to do with your parents' decision to give you this or that name—giving names being a human affair, after all.

Geneva on the Lake

What would Rousseau have to say about this *faux* Geneva—more Stoic, more native, more tribal—were he to return and rewrite the *Social Contract*?

Julia Livilla upstate

Here, at last, Seneca would have been
permitted to indulge his love for the em-
peror's niece—a coarser, more rugged
love—his chin turned toward Rome, his
heart moored to Dresden, his grim future
buried in Moscow.

For Durs Grünbein

On the longevity of art

"Life is short, but art endures," they say. This is a false opposition, as art endures only to the extent that it has been infused with life. This means not only that art and life are never less than coterminous, but that, if anything, life outlives art and not the other way around.

More often than not, we don't gain anything by being right. In the best case, it is redundant—in the worst case, it makes us look self-righteous and arrogant. Often, being wrong is preferable to being right —at least we can learn something from it.

On "I didn't mean it"

Often, when we say "I didn't mean it" we are disingenuous, for we did mean to say what we now say we didn't mean when we said it. Often, "I didn't mean it" really means "I wish I hadn't meant it."

ON FRIENDS

A friend not only wants you to be well and do well, but he is actually happy with you when you are doing well.

~

It is often easier to offer sympathy and support to a friend in need than to celebrate a friend's prosperity and successes without envy.

~

Like love, friendship is not based on need.

Genuine novelty is rare. Most of the time, novelty means that we have forgotten to remember that in one way or another it has been said or done before.

ON FIRSTS IN PHILOSOPHY

Aristotle's metaphysics, Descartes' meth-
od of doubt, Edmund Husserl's logic,
Emmanuel Levinas' ethics—all self-pro-
claimed *First Philosophies*. Which one, now,
is actually first?

    —in response to Descartes' silent debt to
Aristotle's *Metaphysics* 1005b-1006a, 1011a-b

ON NONVIOLENT COMMUNICATION

"Efface the thought, I am harmed, and at once the feeling of being harmed disappears; efface the feeling and the harm disappears at once."

(Marcus Aurelius, *Meditations*, book 4, 7)

For Marshall B. Rosenberg

America

The memory of a promise in the future perfect.

On Revenge, *More Cynico*

When asked how one should avenge oneself on one's enemies, Diogenes replied: by behaving like a gentleman. Similarly, Marcus Aurelius advised that the best way of avenging oneself is not to do likewise.

~

Harboring thoughts of revenge poisons your life. The unexpected gift of revenge undesired is sweet.

On Genius

Genius, J. W. Goethe once said, is the power to compel a critic to alter his judgment.

~

When I think of genius, I think of the ocean: breakers leaving no marks, small waves pleasant to behold and dip into, tall waves that challenge without threat, tidal waves that destroy and remake—stormy at times, and calm—unpredictable, always, and always a temptation.

Recently, my teenage son began writing aphorisms. One, in particular, strikes me as a perfect exemplar of the genre: "Often, when an adult underestimates a child's intelligence, he actually overestimates his own."

On simplicity without simplification

A misguided "love of simplicity," David Hume remarks, "has been the source of much false reasoning."

~

Sometimes, keeping it simple will actually complicate things. The trick is to make it simple without simplifying it.

On a Lamprey

In his famous letter to Francis Bacon, Lord Chandos makes reference to an episode in the life of Crassus the orator, "of whom it is reported that he grew so immeasurably fond of a tame lamprey—a dull, dumb, red-eyed fish in his ornamental pond—that it became the talk of the town." And when "one day in the senate Domitius reproached him for shedding tears over the death of his fish, aiming thereby to make him appear a fool, Crassus replied, 'Thus I have done over the death of my fish as you have done over the death of neither your first nor your second wife'."

"I cannot tell you," Lord Chandos continues, "how often this Crassus with his lamprey enters my mind … and not so much on account of his reply to Domitius, which may have brought the laughs on his side … for even if Domitius had shed bitter tears of the most sincere sorrow over his wives, there would still be Crassus with his tears over his fish."

"And on this figure, so ridiculous and contemptible in the midst of a world-ruling senate engaged in debating matters most sublime," Lord Chandos concludes, "I am compelled, by a power unknown, to reflect …"

~

Trivial, in its very provocation, as the moral of the story of Crassus and his lamprey may be—to wit: life and death, having absolute value, admit (as Crassus knows and Chandos suspects) of no axiological ranking—it does bear retelling: too often, we act Domitius' part.

For Louie Free

If it is true, as Max Scheler suggests, that "evidently nobody ever becomes 'good' through ethics," then why do we continue pursuing it?—Evidently, we have a deep-seated need to chronicle our moral insufficiencies by continuing to imagine what we ought to be.

ON BEING A PHILOSOPHER

—the courage to think for yourself—the
passion completely to dedicate yourself to
it —the perseverance to carry it through
to the end—

On Love II

"While you live, you have to want to die with him—when he dies, you have to want to live for him.

~

While you live, you have to want to die with her—when she dies, you have to want to live for her."

(Kathrin Stengel)

On marrying for money

If you marry for money, sooner or later you'll have to pay for it.

ON INTELLIGENCE AND GENIUS

"Learning from your own mistakes is intelligence; learning from the mistakes of others—genius."

(Elias Stengel-Eskin)

On winning and losing

If you lose the will to win, you've already lost.

For Ronald Dillard

On Wanting Children

We often want to have children without
wanting to be parents.

ON REPUBLICANS AND DEMOCRATS

"The difference between Republicans and Democrats is that Republicans want to govern, while Democrats want government."

(Kathrin Stengel)

On the Wrong Side of the Bed

"In a marriage, there's only one bed—so somebody is bound to get up on the wrong side."

(Elias Stengel-Eskin)

On love and responsibility

There is love born of responsibility and there is responsibility born of love. 'Love' that is neither born of nor bears responsibility is mere infatuation.

ON AGING

Up to a certain point in your life, you look the way were. Then, one day, you see yourself in the mirror, and you realize that you look the way you will be.

On what the 'wise man' would do

Asking yourself what the 'wise man' would do in your situation when confronted with a dilemma or problem—as some teachers of philosophy propose—is misguided in at least two respects:

1. If you don't know what you yourself ought to do in your own situation, why would you think that you could possibly divine what another would do, were he—impossibly—in it?

2. Wisdom involves an element of surprise—the 'wise man' is one who thinks outside the box, his actions are not chartable in advance—if they were, he would merely be prudent, not wise.

Among other things, the prenuptial agreement between the young Mary, Queen of Scots, and her first husband, Francis II, the Dauphin of France, stipulates that the groom receive the so-called "matrimonial crown," thus automatically becoming King of Scotland by marriage, and that the bride bequeath Scotland to France in case she should die prematurely or without an heir.

"This agreement is mendacious from the start," Stefan Zweig writes in his biography of Mary Stuart, "for it is not at all within Mary's legal purview to arbitrarily tamper with her family's line of succession and leave her country to another dynasty after her death as though it were a piece of clothing or chattel. Her as-of-yet ignorant hand appends the signature under pressure from the distaff—French—side of her family."

Thus, Zweig observes, "Mary's very first signature of political consequence is also the first big lie that this deeply honest, trusting, and transparent soul perpetrates; in order to remain Queen, she will henceforth no longer be able ever to act in complete honesty."

~

"For he who has indentured himself to politics," Zweig wistfully concludes, "no longer belongs to himself and must obey laws other than the sacred ones governing his inner nature ... A powerful lie costs the cunning politician no more than a breath of hollow air."

ON OBSERVING WITHOUT JUDGING

Is it truly possible to observe without judging, as some have suggested?

If all seeing is perspectival, as Nietzsche observes, and if perspective necessarily implies selection, focus, and omission; and if observing is a particular kind of seeing that chooses to home in on *this* rather than *that*, which it leaves out of focus; and if *homing in* is premised on *this* being given priority over *that*—and this means being assigned a higher value (if only for the duration of observation)—then observing would not seem to be possible without judging, insofar as the very question of value by definition implies judgment: right/wrong, not guilty/

guilty, beautiful/ugly, healthy/unhealthy, etc., all of which in turn are governed by the most fundamental value distinction: good/bad, good/evil. Observing, then, would—however tenuously and imperceptibly—always already be tethered to the latter, structurally unable to escape its framework.

~

Even detachment—if indeed it be truly possible—would still be a form of judging: namely, the (lack of) importance of (our involvement in) *this* or *that*, its not *meriting* our investment ... putting our wellbeing, our inner peace first ...

—with J. Krishnamurti in mind

About the Author

An award-winning philosophers, author, translator, literary critic, and publisher, MICHAEL ESKIN has taught at the University of Cambridge and Columbia University. His essays, reviews, and translations have appeared in *The New Yorker*, *TLS*, and *World Literature Today*, among other venues. His books include: *Ethics and Dialogue in the Works of Levinas, Bakhtin, Mandelshtam, and Celan*; *Poetic Affairs: Celan, Grünbein, Brodsky*; *The DNA of Prejudice*; *Yoga for the Mind*; and *The Wisdom of Parenthood*. He has been a frequent guest on radio programs and lectured regularly on cultural, philosophical, and literary subjects across the US and Europe—as a guest of, PEN, the United States Consulate General, Germany, The Federation of German-American Clubs, and Limmud, an international organization fostering cross-cultural Jewish education, among others. He lives in New York City.

Available from UWSP

- *November Rose: A Speech on Death*
  by Kathrin Stengel (2008 Independent
  Publisher Book Award)
- *November-Rose: Eine Rede über den Tod*
  by Kathrin Stengel
- *Philosophical Fragments of a Contemporary Life*
  by Julien David
- *17 Vorurteile, die wir Deutschen gegen Amerika und
  die Amerikaner haben und die so nicht ganz
  stimmen können* by Misha Waiman
- *The DNA of Prejudice: On the One and the
  Many* by Michael Eskin (2010 Next Generation
  Indie Book Award for Social Change)
- *Descartes' Devil: Three Meditations*
  by Durs Grünbein
- *Fatal Numbers: Why Count on Chance*
  by Hans Magnus Enzensberger
- *The Vocation of Poetry* by Durs Grünbein
  (2011 Independent Publisher Book Award)
- *The Waiting Game: An Essay on the Gift of Time*
  by Andrea Köhler (out of print)
- *Mortal Diamond: Poems* by Durs Grünbein

- *Yoga for the Mind: A New Ethic for Thinking and Being & Meridians of Thought* by Michael Eskin & Kathrin Stengel (2014 Living Now Book Award)
- *The Wisdom of Parenthood: An Essay* by Michael Eskin
- *Health is in Your Hands: Jin Shin Jyutsu – Practicing the Art of Self-Healing (With 51 Flash Cards for the Hands-On Practice of Jin Shin Jyutsu)* by Waltraud Riegger-Krause (2015 Living Now Book Award for Healing Arts)
- *A Moment More Sublime: A Novel* by Stephen Grant (2015 Independent Publisher Book Award)
- *High on Low: Harnessing the Power of Unhappiness* by Wilhelm Schmid (2015 Living Now Book Award for Personal Growth)
- *Become a Message: Poems* by Lajos Walder (2016 Benjamin Franklin Award)
- *What We Gain As We Grow Older: On Gelassenheit* by Wilhelm Schmid (2016 Living Now Book Award)
- *On Dialogic Speech* by L. P. Yakubinsky
- *Tyrtaeus: A Tragedy* by Lajos Walder
- *Vase of Pompeii: A Play* by Lajos Walder
- *Below Zero: A Play* by Lajos Walder

- *The Complete Plays of Lajos Walder* by Lajos Walder
- *Passing Time: An Essay on Waiting* by Andrea Köhler
- *In Praise of Weakness* by Alexandre Jollien
- *Homo Conscius: A Novel* by Timothy Balding
- *Spanish Light: A Novel* by Stephen Grant
- *On Language & Poetry: Three Essays* by L. P. Yakubinsky
- *Philosophical Truffles* by Michael Eskin
- *The Impostors: A Novel* by Timothy Balding (forthcoming)
- *The Complete Poetry of Lajos Walder: A Bilingual Edition* by Lajos Walder (forthcoming)
- *Potentially Harmless: A Philosopher's Manhattan* by Kathrin Stengel (forthcoming)
- *Of Parents and Children: Tools for Nurturing a Fundamental Relationship* by Jorge and Demián Bucay (forthcoming)

Designed by UWSP
Printed in the United States of America

Made in the USA
Monee, IL
17 March 2026

46281833R00062